M Y P
BLUE-TONGUE

THIS BOOK BELONGS TO:

ALL ABOUT YOUR SKINK

PHOTO/DRAWING

NAME:

DOB:

BREED/COLOR:

SEX:

COLOR & MARKING:

LINCENSE #:

ADOPTION PLACE:

SPECIES:

MICROCHIP:

HOW WE MET:

HOW HE/HER GOT NAME:

OWNER'S INFORMATION

NAME:

ADDRESS:

PHONE: EMAIL:

VET INFORMATION

CLINIC: VET:

ADDRESS:

PHONE: EMAIL:

IMPORTANT NUMBERS

NAME:	PHONE:	ADDRESS:

NOTES:
- ●
- ●
- ●

MEDICATION RECORD/VET VISITS

DATE: REASON FOR VISIT: NEXT VISIT:

DATE: REASON FOR VISIT: NEXT VISIT:

DATE: REASON FOR VISIT: NEXT VISIT:

DATE: REASON FOR VISIT: NEXT VISIT:

DATE: REASON FOR VISIT: NEXT VISIT:

DATE: REASON FOR VISIT: NEXT VISIT:

DATE: REASON FOR VISIT: NEXT VISIT:

GROWTH CHART

DATE	WEIGHT	DATE	WEIGHT

GROWTH CHART

DATE	WEIGHT	DATE	WEIGHT

ABOUT AFRICAN BULLFROG

LIFE SPAN

- 10 years

SIZE

- 8 -10 inches long

HUMIDITY

- 80% to 90%

HEAT & LIGHT

- A room that doesn't drop below 75 degrees Fahrenheit
- 12 hours of light and 12 hours of darkness each day

Daily, Weekly & Monthly Activity

Daily Activity

 Feed Blue-tongue skink every 2-3 days

 Clean and refresh water bowl

 Check temperatures Check & hydrate humid are if required

 Spot clean any waste Remove any uneaten food

 Visually inspect tortoise

Every Other Day Activity

 Use calcium supplements

Weekly Activity

 Clean glass

 Top up substrate

 Clean any decorative rocks, plants etc

 Physically inspect Tortoise

 Weigh Tortoise & record data

Monthly Activity

 Remove & replace all substrate

DAILY CHECKLIST

Daily Activity	WEEK OF						
	SUN	MON	TUE	WED	THU	FRI	SAT
Feed Skink	○	○	○	○	○	○	○
Clean & refresh water bowl	○	○	○	○	○	○	○
Check temp / humidity	○	○	○	○	○	○	○
Clean waste Remove uneaten food	○	○	○	○	○	○	○
Visually inspect.	○	○	○	○	○	○	○
Use calcium supplements 1 x / 2-3 day	○	○	○	○	○	○	○

NOTES:

WEEKLY CHECKLIST

WEEK OF _____

WEEKLY ACTIVITY

- ○ Clean glass
- ○ Top up substrate
- ○ Clean any decorative rocks, plants etc
- ○ Physically inspect
- ○ Weigh & record data
- ○ _____

MONTHLY ACTIVITY

- ○ Remove & replace all substrate

HEALTH CHECKLIST

- ○ Active and alert
- ○ Eats regularly
- ○ Clear, bright eyes
- ○ Healthy skin
- ○ Clear nose and vent

NOTES:

HIGHLIGHT OF THE WEEK:

DAILY CHECKLIST

Daily Activity	WEEK OF						
	SUN	MON	TUE	WED	THU	FRI	SAT
Feed Skink	○	○	○	○	○	○	○
Clean & refresh water bowl	○	○	○	○	○	○	○
Check temp / humidity	○	○	○	○	○	○	○
Clean waste Remove uneaten food	○	○	○	○	○	○	○
Visually inspect.	○	○	○	○	○	○	○
Use calcium supplements 1 x / 2-3 day	○	○	○	○	○	○	○

NOTES:

WEEKLY CHECKLIST

WEEK OF [   ]

WEEKLY ACTIVITY

○ Clean glass

○ Top up substrate

○ Clean any decorative rocks, plants etc

○ Physically inspect

○ Weigh & record data

[   ]

MONTHLY ACTIVITY

○ Remove & replace all substrate

HEALTH CHECKLIST

○ Active and alert

○ Eats regularly

○ Clear, bright eyes

○ Healthy skin

○ Clear nose and vent

NOTES:

HIGHLIGHT OF THE WEEK:

DAILY CHECKLIST

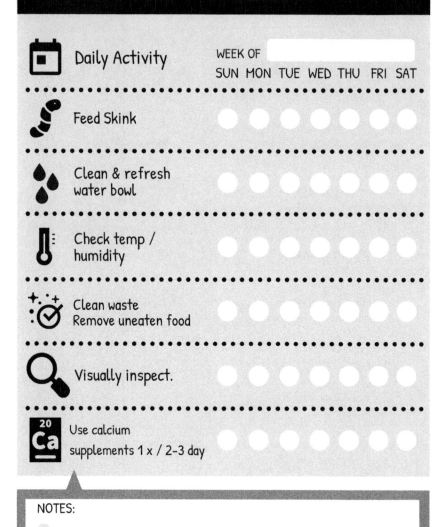

Daily Activity	WEEK OF	SUN	MON	TUE	WED	THU	FRI	SAT
Feed Skink		○	○	○	○	○	○	○
Clean & refresh water bowl		○	○	○	○	○	○	○
Check temp / humidity		○	○	○	○	○	○	○
Clean waste Remove uneaten food		○	○	○	○	○	○	○
Visually inspect.		○	○	○	○	○	○	○
Use calcium supplements 1 x / 2-3 day		○	○	○	○	○	○	○

NOTES:

WEEKLY CHECKLIST

WEEK OF _____

WEEKLY ACTIVITY

- ○ Clean glass
- ○ Top up substrate
- ○ Clean any decorative rocks, plants etc
- ○ Physically inspect
- ○ Weigh & record data
- _____

MONTHLY ACTIVITY

- ○ Remove & replace all substrate

HEALTH CHECKLIST

- ○ Active and alert
- ○ Eats regularly
- ○ Clear, bright eyes
- ○ Healthy skin
- ○ Clear nose and vent

NOTES:

HIGHLIGHT OF THE WEEK:

DAILY CHECKLIST

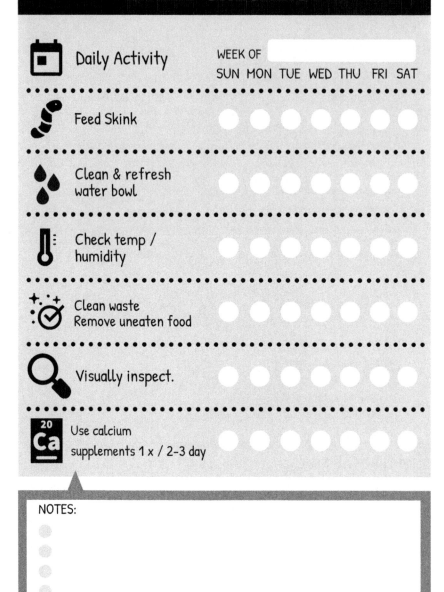

Daily Activity	WEEK OF	SUN	MON	TUE	WED	THU	FRI	SAT
Feed Skink		○	○	○	○	○	○	○
Clean & refresh water bowl		○	○	○	○	○	○	○
Check temp / humidity		○	○	○	○	○	○	○
Clean waste Remove uneaten food		○	○	○	○	○	○	○
Visually inspect.		○	○	○	○	○	○	○
Use calcium supplements 1 x / 2-3 day		○	○	○	○	○	○	○

NOTES:

WEEKLY CHECKLIST

WEEK OF [   ]

WEEKLY ACTIVITY

- ○ Clean glass
- ○ Top up substrate
- ○ Clean any decorative rocks, plants etc
- ○ Physically inspect
- ○ Weigh & record data

[   ]

MONTHLY ACTIVITY

- ○ Remove & replace all substrate

HEALTH CHECKLIST

- ○ Active and alert
- ○ Eats regularly
- ○ Clear, bright eyes
- ○ Healthy skin
- ○ Clear nose and vent

NOTES:

HIGHLIGHT OF THE WEEK:

DAILY CHECKLIST

Daily Activity	WEEK OF						
	SUN	MON	TUE	WED	THU	FRI	SAT
Feed Skink	○	○	○	○	○	○	○
Clean & refresh water bowl	○	○	○	○	○	○	○
Check temp / humidity	○	○	○	○	○	○	○
Clean waste Remove uneaten food	○	○	○	○	○	○	○
Visually inspect.	○	○	○	○	○	○	○
Use calcium supplements 1 x / 2-3 day	○	○	○	○	○	○	○

NOTES:

WEEKLY CHECKLIST

WEEK OF _____

WEEKLY ACTIVITY

- ○ Clean glass
- ○ Top up substrate
- ○ Clean any decorative rocks, plants etc
- ○ Physically inspect
- ○ Weigh & record data
- ○ _____

MONTHLY ACTIVITY

- ○ Remove & replace all substrate

HEALTH CHECKLIST

- ○ Active and alert
- ○ Eats regularly
- ○ Clear, bright eyes
- ○ Healthy skin
- ○ Clear nose and vent

NOTES:

HIGHLIGHT OF THE WEEK:

DAILY CHECKLIST

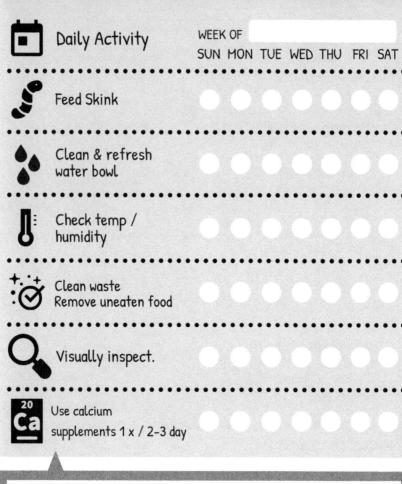

📅 Daily Activity

WEEK OF ☐

SUN MON TUE WED THU FRI SAT

Feed Skink ○ ○ ○ ○ ○ ○ ○

Clean & refresh
water bowl ○ ○ ○ ○ ○ ○ ○

Check temp /
humidity ○ ○ ○ ○ ○ ○ ○

Clean waste
Remove uneaten food ○ ○ ○ ○ ○ ○ ○

Visually inspect. ○ ○ ○ ○ ○ ○ ○

20 Ca Use calcium
supplements 1 x / 2-3 day ○ ○ ○ ○ ○ ○ ○

NOTES:

WEEKLY CHECKLIST

WEEK OF [   ]

WEEKLY ACTIVITY

- ○ Clean glass
- ○ Top up substrate
- ○ Clean any decorative rocks, plants etc
- ○ Physically inspect
- ○ Weigh & record data
  [   ]

MONTHLY ACTIVITY

- ○ Remove & replace all substrate

HEALTH CHECKLIST

- ○ Active and alert
- ○ Eats regularly
- ○ Clear, bright eyes
- ○ Healthy skin
- ○ Clear nose and vent

NOTES:

HIGHLIGHT OF THE WEEK:

DAILY CHECKLIST

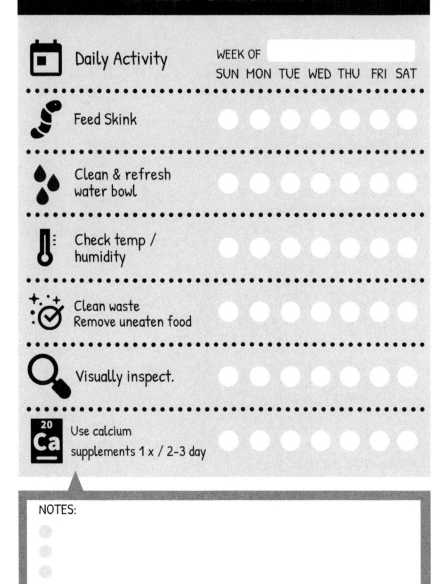

Daily Activity	WEEK OF	SUN	MON	TUE	WED	THU	FRI	SAT
Feed Skink		○	○	○	○	○	○	○
Clean & refresh water bowl		○	○	○	○	○	○	○
Check temp / humidity		○	○	○	○	○	○	○
Clean waste Remove uneaten food		○	○	○	○	○	○	○
Visually inspect.		○	○	○	○	○	○	○
Use calcium supplements 1 x / 2-3 day		○	○	○	○	○	○	○

NOTES:

WEEKLY CHECKLIST

WEEK OF

WEEKLY ACTIVITY

- ◯ Clean glass
- ◯ Top up substrate
- ◯ Clean any decorative rocks, plants etc
- ◯ Physically inspect
- ◯ Weigh & record data

MONTHLY ACTIVITY

- ◯ Remove & replace all substrate

HEALTH CHECKLIST

- ◯ Active and alert
- ◯ Eats regularly
- ◯ Clear, bright eyes
- ◯ Healthy skin
- ◯ Clear nose and vent

NOTES:

HIGHLIGHT OF THE WEEK:

DAILY CHECKLIST

Daily Activity	WEEK OF						
	SUN	MON	TUE	WED	THU	FRI	SAT
Feed Skink	○	○	○	○	○	○	○
Clean & refresh water bowl	○	○	○	○	○	○	○
Check temp / humidity	○	○	○	○	○	○	○
Clean waste Remove uneaten food	○	○	○	○	○	○	○
Visually inspect.	○	○	○	○	○	○	○
Use calcium supplements 1 x / 2-3 day	○	○	○	○	○	○	○

NOTES:

WEEKLY CHECKLIST

WEEK OF

WEEKLY ACTIVITY

- Clean glass
- Top up substrate
- Clean any decorative rocks, plants etc
- Physically inspect
- Weigh & record data

MONTHLY ACTIVITY

- Remove & replace all substrate

HEALTH CHECKLIST

- Active and alert
- Eats regularly
- Clear, bright eyes
- Healthy skin
- Clear nose and vent

NOTES:

HIGHLIGHT OF THE WEEK:

DAILY CHECKLIST

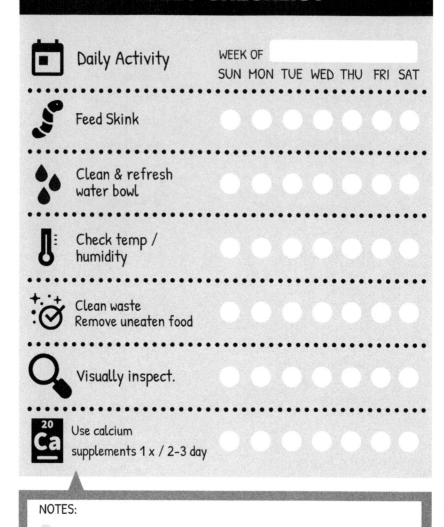

Daily Activity	WEEK OF	SUN	MON	TUE	WED	THU	FRI	SAT
Feed Skink		○	○	○	○	○	○	○
Clean & refresh water bowl		○	○	○	○	○	○	○
Check temp / humidity		○	○	○	○	○	○	○
Clean waste Remove uneaten food		○	○	○	○	○	○	○
Visually inspect.		○	○	○	○	○	○	○
Use calcium supplements 1 x / 2-3 day		○	○	○	○	○	○	○

NOTES:

WEEKLY CHECKLIST

WEEK OF

WEEKLY ACTIVITY

- Clean glass
- Top up substrate
- Clean any decorative rocks, plants etc
- Physically inspect
- Weigh & record data

MONTHLY ACTIVITY

- Remove & replace all substrate

HEALTH CHECKLIST

- Active and alert
- Eats regularly
- Clear, bright eyes
- Healthy skin
- Clear nose and vent

NOTES:

HIGHLIGHT OF THE WEEK:

DAILY CHECKLIST

Daily Activity	WEEK OF	SUN	MON	TUE	WED	THU	FRI	SAT
Feed Skink		○	○	○	○	○	○	○
Clean & refresh water bowl		○	○	○	○	○	○	○
Check temp / humidity		○	○	○	○	○	○	○
Clean waste Remove uneaten food		○	○	○	○	○	○	○
Visually inspect.		○	○	○	○	○	○	○
Use calcium supplements 1 x / 2-3 day		○	○	○	○	○	○	○

NOTES:

WEEKLY CHECKLIST

WEEK OF

WEEKLY ACTIVITY

- ⚪ Clean glass
- ⚪ Top up substrate
- ⚪ Clean any decorative rocks, plants etc
- ⚪ Physically inspect
- ⚪ Weigh & record data

MONTHLY ACTIVITY

- ⚪ Remove & replace all substrate

HEALTH CHECKLIST

- ⚪ Active and alert
- ⚪ Eats regularly
- ⚪ Clear, bright eyes
- ⚪ Healthy skin
- ⚪ Clear nose and vent

NOTES:

HIGHLIGHT OF THE WEEK:

DAILY CHECKLIST

📅 Daily Activity

WEEK OF _____

	SUN	MON	TUE	WED	THU	FRI	SAT
Feed Skink	○	○	○	○	○	○	○
Clean & refresh water bowl	○	○	○	○	○	○	○
Check temp / humidity	○	○	○	○	○	○	○
Clean waste Remove uneaten food	○	○	○	○	○	○	○
Visually inspect.	○	○	○	○	○	○	○
Ca 20 Use calcium supplements 1 x / 2-3 day	○	○	○	○	○	○	○

NOTES:

WEEKLY CHECKLIST

WEEK OF _____

WEEKLY ACTIVITY

- ○ Clean glass
- ○ Top up substrate
- ○ Clean any decorative rocks, plants etc
- ○ Physically inspect
- ○ Weigh & record data
  _____

MONTHLY ACTIVITY

- ○ Remove & replace all substrate

HEALTH CHECKLIST

- ○ Active and alert
- ○ Eats regularly
- ○ Clear, bright eyes
- ○ Healthy skin
- ○ Clear nose and vent

NOTES:

HIGHLIGHT OF THE WEEK:

DAILY CHECKLIST

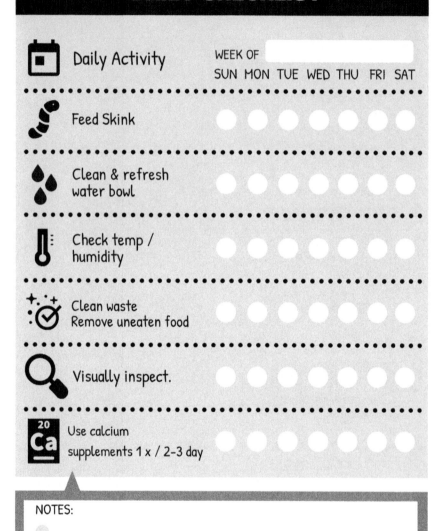

Daily Activity	WEEK OF
	SUN MON TUE WED THU FRI SAT
Feed Skink	○ ○ ○ ○ ○ ○ ○
Clean & refresh water bowl	○ ○ ○ ○ ○ ○ ○
Check temp / humidity	○ ○ ○ ○ ○ ○ ○
Clean waste Remove uneaten food	○ ○ ○ ○ ○ ○ ○
Visually inspect.	○ ○ ○ ○ ○ ○ ○
²⁰Ca Use calcium supplements 1 x / 2-3 day	○ ○ ○ ○ ○ ○ ○

NOTES:

WEEKLY CHECKLIST

WEEK OF

WEEKLY ACTIVITY

- Clean glass
- Top up substrate
- Clean any decorative rocks, plants etc
- Physically inspect
- Weigh & record data

MONTHLY ACTIVITY

- Remove & replace all substrate

HEALTH CHECKLIST

- Active and alert
- Eats regularly
- Clear, bright eyes
- Healthy skin
- Clear nose and vent

NOTES:

HIGHLIGHT OF THE WEEK:

DAILY CHECKLIST

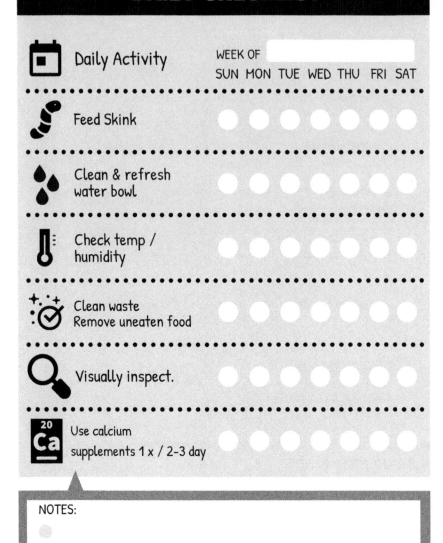

Daily Activity

WEEK OF

	SUN	MON	TUE	WED	THU	FRI	SAT
Feed Skink	○	○	○	○	○	○	○
Clean & refresh water bowl	○	○	○	○	○	○	○
Check temp / humidity	○	○	○	○	○	○	○
Clean waste Remove uneaten food	○	○	○	○	○	○	○
Visually inspect.	○	○	○	○	○	○	○
Use calcium supplements 1 x / 2-3 day	○	○	○	○	○	○	○

NOTES:

WEEKLY CHECKLIST

WEEK OF

WEEKLY ACTIVITY

- Clean glass
- Top up substrate
- Clean any decorative rocks, plants etc
- Physically inspect
- Weigh & record data

MONTHLY ACTIVITY

- Remove & replace all substrate

HEALTH CHECKLIST

- Active and alert
- Eats regularly
- Clear, bright eyes
- Healthy skin
- Clear nose and vent

NOTES:

HIGHLIGHT OF THE WEEK:

DAILY CHECKLIST

Daily Activity	SUN	MON	TUE	WED	THU	FRI	SAT
WEEK OF							
Feed Skink	○	○	○	○	○	○	○
Clean & refresh water bowl	○	○	○	○	○	○	○
Check temp / humidity	○	○	○	○	○	○	○
Clean waste Remove uneaten food	○	○	○	○	○	○	○
Visually inspect.	○	○	○	○	○	○	○
Use calcium supplements 1 x / 2-3 day	○	○	○	○	○	○	○

NOTES:

WEEKLY CHECKLIST

WEEK OF [   ]

WEEKLY ACTIVITY

- ○ Clean glass
- ○ Top up substrate
- ○ Clean any decorative rocks, plants etc
- ○ Physically inspect
- ○ Weigh & record data
  [   ]

MONTHLY ACTIVITY

- ○ Remove & replace all substrate

HEALTH CHECKLIST

- ○ Active and alert
- ○ Eats regularly
- ○ Clear, bright eyes
- ○ Healthy skin
- ○ Clear nose and vent

NOTES:

HIGHLIGHT OF THE WEEK:

DAILY CHECKLIST

Daily Activity

WEEK OF

SUN MON TUE WED THU FRI SAT

Feed Skink

Clean & refresh water bowl

Check temp / humidity

Clean waste Remove uneaten food

Visually inspect.

Use calcium supplements 1 x / 2-3 day

NOTES:

WEEKLY CHECKLIST

WEEK OF

WEEKLY ACTIVITY

- ○ Clean glass
- ○ Top up substrate
- ○ Clean any decorative rocks, plants etc
- ○ Physically inspect
- ○ Weigh & record data

MONTHLY ACTIVITY

- ○ Remove & replace all substrate

HEALTH CHECKLIST

- ○ Active and alert
- ○ Eats regularly
- ○ Clear, bright eyes
- ○ Healthy skin
- ○ Clear nose and vent

NOTES:

HIGHLIGHT OF THE WEEK:

DAILY CHECKLIST

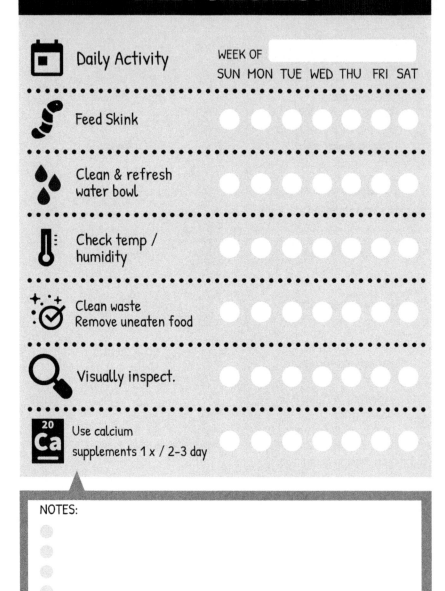

Daily Activity	WEEK OF						
	SUN	MON	TUE	WED	THU	FRI	SAT
Feed Skink	○	○	○	○	○	○	○
Clean & refresh water bowl	○	○	○	○	○	○	○
Check temp / humidity	○	○	○	○	○	○	○
Clean waste Remove uneaten food	○	○	○	○	○	○	○
Visually inspect.	○	○	○	○	○	○	○
Use calcium supplements 1 x / 2-3 day	○	○	○	○	○	○	○

NOTES:

WEEKLY CHECKLIST

WEEK OF [_____]

WEEKLY ACTIVITY

- ○ Clean glass
- ○ Top up substrate
- ○ Clean any decorative rocks, plants etc
- ○ Physically inspect
- ○ Weigh & record data
  [_____]

MONTHLY ACTIVITY

- ○ Remove & replace all substrate

HEALTH CHECKLIST

- ○ Active and alert
- ○ Eats regularly
- ○ Clear, bright eyes
- ○ Healthy skin
- ○ Clear nose and vent

NOTES:

HIGHLIGHT OF THE WEEK:

DAILY CHECKLIST

Daily Activity	WEEK OF						
	SUN	MON	TUE	WED	THU	FRI	SAT
Feed Skink	○	○	○	○	○	○	○
Clean & refresh water bowl	○	○	○	○	○	○	○
Check temp / humidity	○	○	○	○	○	○	○
Clean waste Remove uneaten food	○	○	○	○	○	○	○
Visually inspect.	○	○	○	○	○	○	○
Use calcium supplements 1 x / 2-3 day	○	○	○	○	○	○	○

NOTES:

WEEKLY CHECKLIST

WEEK OF

WEEKLY ACTIVITY

- Clean glass
- Top up substrate
- Clean any decorative rocks, plants etc
- Physically inspect
- Weigh & record data

MONTHLY ACTIVITY

- Remove & replace all substrate

HEALTH CHECKLIST

- Active and alert
- Eats regularly
- Clear, bright eyes
- Healthy skin
- Clear nose and vent

NOTES:

HIGHLIGHT OF THE WEEK:

DAILY CHECKLIST

Daily Activity	WEEK OF	SUN	MON	TUE	WED	THU	FRI	SAT
Feed Skink		○	○	○	○	○	○	○
Clean & refresh water bowl		○	○	○	○	○	○	○
Check temp / humidity		○	○	○	○	○	○	○
Clean waste Remove uneaten food		○	○	○	○	○	○	○
Visually inspect.		○	○	○	○	○	○	○
Use calcium supplements 1 x / 2-3 day		○	○	○	○	○	○	○

NOTES:

WEEKLY CHECKLIST

WEEK OF

WEEKLY ACTIVITY

○ Clean glass

○ Top up substrate

○ Clean any decorative rocks, plants etc

○ Physically inspect

○ Weigh & record data

MONTHLY ACTIVITY

○ Remove & replace all substrate

HEALTH CHECKLIST

○ Active and alert

○ Eats regularly

○ Clear, bright eyes

○ Healthy skin

○ Clear nose and vent

NOTES:

HIGHLIGHT OF THE WEEK:

DAILY CHECKLIST

Daily Activity	WEEK OF	SUN	MON	TUE	WED	THU	FRI	SAT
Feed Skink		○	○	○	○	○	○	○
Clean & refresh water bowl		○	○	○	○	○	○	○
Check temp / humidity		○	○	○	○	○	○	○
Clean waste Remove uneaten food		○	○	○	○	○	○	○
Visually inspect.		○	○	○	○	○	○	○
Use calcium supplements 1 x / 2-3 day		○	○	○	○	○	○	○

NOTES:

WEEKLY CHECKLIST

WEEK OF _____

WEEKLY ACTIVITY

- ◯ Clean glass
- ◯ Top up substrate
- ◯ Clean any decorative rocks, plants etc
- ◯ Physically inspect
- ◯ Weigh & record data
  _____

MONTHLY ACTIVITY

- ◯ Remove & replace all substrate

HEALTH CHECKLIST

- ◯ Active and alert
- ◯ Eats regularly
- ◯ Clear, bright eyes
- ◯ Healthy skin
- ◯ Clear nose and vent

NOTES:

HIGHLIGHT OF THE WEEK:

DAILY CHECKLIST

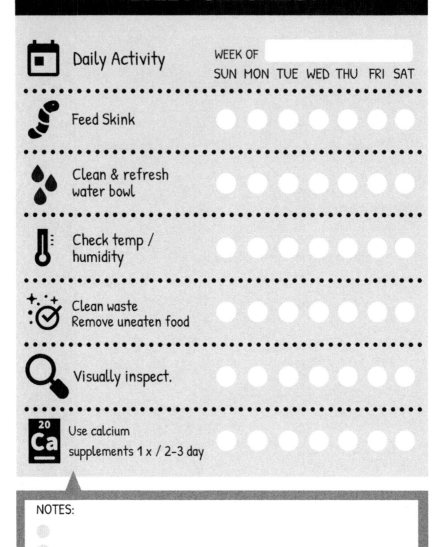

Daily Activity	WEEK OF						
	SUN	MON	TUE	WED	THU	FRI	SAT
Feed Skink	○	○	○	○	○	○	○
Clean & refresh water bowl	○	○	○	○	○	○	○
Check temp / humidity	○	○	○	○	○	○	○
Clean waste Remove uneaten food	○	○	○	○	○	○	○
Visually inspect.	○	○	○	○	○	○	○
Use calcium supplements 1 x / 2-3 day	○	○	○	○	○	○	○

NOTES:

WEEKLY CHECKLIST

WEEK OF _____

WEEKLY ACTIVITY

○ Clean glass

○ Top up substrate

○ Clean any decorative rocks, plants etc

○ Physically inspect

○ Weigh & record data

_____

MONTHLY ACTIVITY

○ Remove & replace all substrate

HEALTH CHECKLIST

○ Active and alert

○ Eats regularly

○ Clear, bright eyes

○ Healthy skin

○ Clear nose and vent

NOTES:

HIGHLIGHT OF THE WEEK:

DAILY CHECKLIST

Daily Activity	WEEK OF						
	SUN	MON	TUE	WED	THU	FRI	SAT
Feed Skink	○	○	○	○	○	○	○
Clean & refresh water bowl	○	○	○	○	○	○	○
Check temp / humidity	○	○	○	○	○	○	○
Clean waste Remove uneaten food	○	○	○	○	○	○	○
Visually inspect.	○	○	○	○	○	○	○
20 Ca Use calcium supplements 1 x / 2-3 day	○	○	○	○	○	○	○

NOTES:

WEEKLY CHECKLIST

WEEK OF

WEEKLY ACTIVITY

- Clean glass
- Top up substrate
- Clean any decorative rocks, plants etc
- Physically inspect
- Weigh & record data

MONTHLY ACTIVITY

- Remove & replace all substrate

HEALTH CHECKLIST

- Active and alert
- Eats regularly
- Clear, bright eyes
- Healthy skin
- Clear nose and vent

NOTES:

HIGHLIGHT OF THE WEEK:

DAILY CHECKLIST

Daily Activity	WEEK OF						
	SUN	MON	TUE	WED	THU	FRI	SAT
Feed Skink	○	○	○	○	○	○	○
Clean & refresh water bowl	○	○	○	○	○	○	○
Check temp / humidity	○	○	○	○	○	○	○
Clean waste Remove uneaten food	○	○	○	○	○	○	○
Visually inspect.	○	○	○	○	○	○	○
Use calcium supplements 1 x / 2-3 day	○	○	○	○	○	○	○

NOTES:

WEEKLY CHECKLIST

WEEK OF _____

WEEKLY ACTIVITY

- ○ Clean glass
- ○ Top up substrate
- ○ Clean any decorative rocks, plants etc
- ○ Physically inspect
- ○ Weigh & record data
  _____

MONTHLY ACTIVITY

- ○ Remove & replace all substrate

HEALTH CHECKLIST

- ○ Active and alert
- ○ Eats regularly
- ○ Clear, bright eyes
- ○ Healthy skin
- ○ Clear nose and vent

NOTES:

HIGHLIGHT OF THE WEEK:

DAILY CHECKLIST

Daily Activity	WEEK OF						
	SUN	MON	TUE	WED	THU	FRI	SAT
Feed Skink	○	○	○	○	○	○	○
Clean & refresh water bowl	○	○	○	○	○	○	○
Check temp / humidity	○	○	○	○	○	○	○
Clean waste Remove uneaten food	○	○	○	○	○	○	○
Visually inspect.	○	○	○	○	○	○	○
Use calcium supplements 1 x / 2-3 day	○	○	○	○	○	○	○

NOTES:

WEEKLY CHECKLIST

WEEK OF

WEEKLY ACTIVITY

- Clean glass
- Top up substrate
- Clean any decorative rocks, plants etc
- Physically inspect
- Weigh & record data

MONTHLY ACTIVITY

- Remove & replace all substrate

HEALTH CHECKLIST

- Active and alert
- Eats regularly
- Clear, bright eyes
- Healthy skin
- Clear nose and vent

NOTES:

HIGHLIGHT OF THE WEEK:

DAILY CHECKLIST

Daily Activity	WEEK OF						
	SUN	MON	TUE	WED	THU	FRI	SAT
Feed Skink	◯	◯	◯	◯	◯	◯	◯
Clean & refresh water bowl	◯	◯	◯	◯	◯	◯	◯
Check temp / humidity	◯	◯	◯	◯	◯	◯	◯
Clean waste Remove uneaten food	◯	◯	◯	◯	◯	◯	◯
Visually inspect.	◯	◯	◯	◯	◯	◯	◯
Use calcium supplements 1 x / 2-3 day	◯	◯	◯	◯	◯	◯	◯

NOTES:

WEEKLY CHECKLIST

WEEK OF

WEEKLY ACTIVITY

- ○ Clean glass
- ○ Top up substrate
- ○ Clean any decorative rocks, plants etc
- ○ Physically inspect
- ○ Weigh & record data

MONTHLY ACTIVITY

- ○ Remove & replace all substrate

HEALTH CHECKLIST

- ○ Active and alert
- ○ Eats regularly
- ○ Clear, bright eyes
- ○ Healthy skin
- ○ Clear nose and vent

NOTES:

HIGHLIGHT OF THE WEEK:

DAILY CHECKLIST

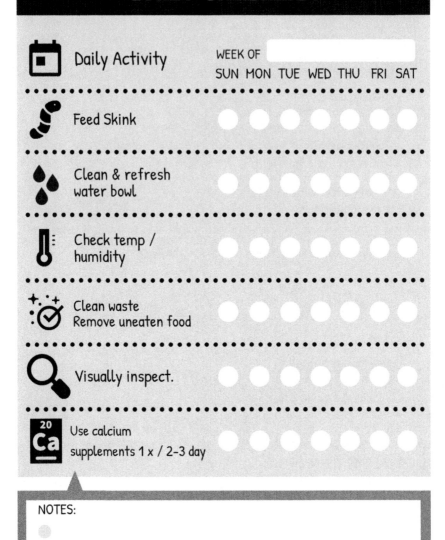

Daily Activity	WEEK OF						
	SUN	MON	TUE	WED	THU	FRI	SAT
Feed Skink	○	○	○	○	○	○	○
Clean & refresh water bowl	○	○	○	○	○	○	○
Check temp / humidity	○	○	○	○	○	○	○
Clean waste Remove uneaten food	○	○	○	○	○	○	○
Visually inspect.	○	○	○	○	○	○	○
Use calcium supplements 1 x / 2-3 day	○	○	○	○	○	○	○

NOTES:

WEEKLY CHECKLIST

WEEK OF

WEEKLY ACTIVITY

- ○ Clean glass
- ○ Top up substrate
- ○ Clean any decorative rocks, plants etc
- ○ Physically inspect
- ○ Weigh & record data

MONTHLY ACTIVITY

- ○ Remove & replace all substrate

HEALTH CHECKLIST

- ○ Active and alert
- ○ Eats regularly
- ○ Clear, bright eyes
- ○ Healthy skin
- ○ Clear nose and vent

NOTES:

HIGHLIGHT OF THE WEEK:

DAILY CHECKLIST

Daily Activity	WEEK OF						
	SUN	MON	TUE	WED	THU	FRI	SAT
Feed Skink	○	○	○	○	○	○	○
Clean & refresh water bowl	○	○	○	○	○	○	○
Check temp / humidity	○	○	○	○	○	○	○
Clean waste Remove uneaten food	○	○	○	○	○	○	○
Visually inspect.	○	○	○	○	○	○	○
20 Ca Use calcium supplements 1 x / 2-3 day	○	○	○	○	○	○	○

NOTES:

WEEKLY CHECKLIST

WEEK OF [   ]

WEEKLY ACTIVITY

- ○ Clean glass
- ○ Top up substrate
- ○ Clean any decorative rocks, plants etc
- ○ Physically inspect
- ○ Weigh & record data
- [   ]

MONTHLY ACTIVITY

- ○ Remove & replace all substrate

HEALTH CHECKLIST

- ○ Active and alert
- ○ Eats regularly
- ○ Clear, bright eyes
- ○ Healthy skin
- ○ Clear nose and vent

NOTES:

HIGHLIGHT OF THE WEEK:

DAILY CHECKLIST

Daily Activity	WEEK OF	SUN	MON	TUE	WED	THU	FRI	SAT
Feed Skink		○	○	○	○	○	○	○
Clean & refresh water bowl		○	○	○	○	○	○	○
Check temp / humidity		○	○	○	○	○	○	○
Clean waste Remove uneaten food		○	○	○	○	○	○	○
Visually inspect.		○	○	○	○	○	○	○
Use calcium supplements 1 x / 2-3 day		○	○	○	○	○	○	○

NOTES:

WEEKLY CHECKLIST

WEEK OF _____

WEEKLY ACTIVITY

- ◯ Clean glass
- ◯ Top up substrate
- ◯ Clean any decorative rocks, plants etc
- ◯ Physically inspect
- ◯ Weigh & record data

MONTHLY ACTIVITY

- ◯ Remove & replace all substrate

HEALTH CHECKLIST

- ◯ Active and alert
- ◯ Eats regularly
- ◯ Clear, bright eyes
- ◯ Healthy skin
- ◯ Clear nose and vent

NOTES:

HIGHLIGHT OF THE WEEK:

DAILY CHECKLIST

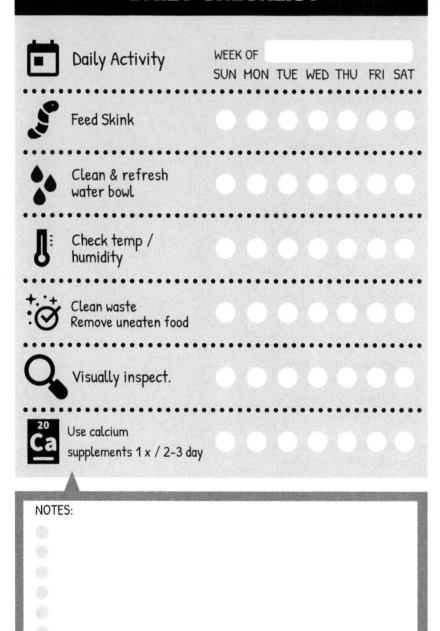

Daily Activity	WEEK OF	SUN	MON	TUE	WED	THU	FRI	SAT
Feed Skink		○	○	○	○	○	○	○
Clean & refresh water bowl		○	○	○	○	○	○	○
Check temp / humidity		○	○	○	○	○	○	○
Clean waste Remove uneaten food		○	○	○	○	○	○	○
Visually inspect.		○	○	○	○	○	○	○
Use calcium supplements 1 x / 2-3 day		○	○	○	○	○	○	○

NOTES:

WEEKLY CHECKLIST

WEEK OF _____

WEEKLY ACTIVITY

- ⚪ Clean glass
- ⚪ Top up substrate
- ⚪ Clean any decorative rocks, plants etc
- ⚪ Physically inspect
- ⚪ Weigh & record data

MONTHLY ACTIVITY

- ⚪ Remove & replace all substrate

HEALTH CHECKLIST

- ⚪ Active and alert
- ⚪ Eats regularly
- ⚪ Clear, bright eyes
- ⚪ Healthy skin
- ⚪ Clear nose and vent

NOTES:

HIGHLIGHT OF THE WEEK:

DAILY CHECKLIST

Daily Activity	WEEK OF	SUN	MON	TUE	WED	THU	FRI	SAT
Feed Skink		○	○	○	○	○	○	○
Clean & refresh water bowl		○	○	○	○	○	○	○
Check temp / humidity		○	○	○	○	○	○	○
Clean waste Remove uneaten food		○	○	○	○	○	○	○
Visually inspect.		○	○	○	○	○	○	○
Use calcium supplements 1 x / 2-3 day		○	○	○	○	○	○	○

NOTES:

WEEKLY CHECKLIST

WEEK OF _____

WEEKLY ACTIVITY

- ○ Clean glass
- ○ Top up substrate
- ○ Clean any decorative rocks, plants etc
- ○ Physically inspect
- ○ Weigh & record data
  _____

MONTHLY ACTIVITY

- ○ Remove & replace all substrate

HEALTH CHECKLIST

- ○ Active and alert
- ○ Eats regularly
- ○ Clear, bright eyes
- ○ Healthy skin
- ○ Clear nose and vent

NOTES:

HIGHLIGHT OF THE WEEK:

DAILY CHECKLIST

Daily Activity	WEEK OF	SUN	MON	TUE	WED	THU	FRI	SAT
Feed Skink		○	○	○	○	○	○	○
Clean & refresh water bowl		○	○	○	○	○	○	○
Check temp / humidity		○	○	○	○	○	○	○
Clean waste Remove uneaten food		○	○	○	○	○	○	○
Visually inspect.		○	○	○	○	○	○	○
Use calcium supplements 1 x / 2-3 day		○	○	○	○	○	○	○

NOTES:

WEEKLY CHECKLIST

WEEK OF

WEEKLY ACTIVITY

- Clean glass
- Top up substrate
- Clean any decorative rocks, plants etc
- Physically inspect
- Weigh & record data

MONTHLY ACTIVITY

- Remove & replace all substrate

HEALTH CHECKLIST

- Active and alert
- Eats regularly
- Clear, bright eyes
- Healthy skin
- Clear nose and vent

NOTES:

HIGHLIGHT OF THE WEEK:

DAILY CHECKLIST

Daily Activity	WEEK OF						
	SUN	MON	TUE	WED	THU	FRI	SAT
Feed Skink	○	○	○	○	○	○	○
Clean & refresh water bowl	○	○	○	○	○	○	○
Check temp / humidity	○	○	○	○	○	○	○
Clean waste Remove uneaten food	○	○	○	○	○	○	○
Visually inspect.	○	○	○	○	○	○	○
Use calcium supplements 1 x / 2-3 day	○	○	○	○	○	○	○

NOTES:

WEEKLY CHECKLIST

WEEK OF

WEEKLY ACTIVITY

○ Clean glass

○ Top up substrate

○ Clean any decorative rocks, plants etc

○ Physically inspect

○ Weigh & record data

MONTHLY ACTIVITY

○ Remove & replace all substrate

HEALTH CHECKLIST

○ Active and alert

○ Eats regularly

○ Clear, bright eyes

○ Healthy skin

○ Clear nose and vent

NOTES:

HIGHLIGHT OF THE WEEK:

DAILY CHECKLIST

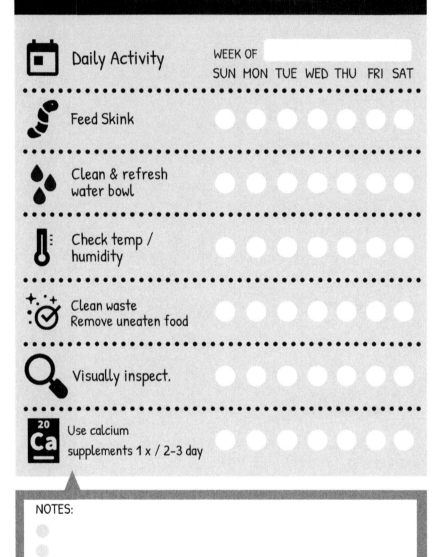

Daily Activity	WEEK OF	SUN	MON	TUE	WED	THU	FRI	SAT
Feed Skink		○	○	○	○	○	○	○
Clean & refresh water bowl		○	○	○	○	○	○	○
Check temp / humidity		○	○	○	○	○	○	○
Clean waste Remove uneaten food		○	○	○	○	○	○	○
Visually inspect.		○	○	○	○	○	○	○
Use calcium supplements 1 x / 2-3 day		○	○	○	○	○	○	○

NOTES:

WEEKLY CHECKLIST

WEEK OF

WEEKLY ACTIVITY

○ Clean glass

○ Top up substrate

○ Clean any decorative rocks, plants etc

○ Physically inspect

○ Weigh & record data

MONTHLY ACTIVITY

○ Remove & replace all substrate

HEALTH CHECKLIST

○ Active and alert

○ Eats regularly

○ Clear, bright eyes

○ Healthy skin

○ Clear nose and vent

NOTES:

HIGHLIGHT OF THE WEEK:

DAILY CHECKLIST

Daily Activity	WEEK OF	SUN	MON	TUE	WED	THU	FRI	SAT
Feed Skink		○	○	○	○	○	○	○
Clean & refresh water bowl		○	○	○	○	○	○	○
Check temp / humidity		○	○	○	○	○	○	○
Clean waste Remove uneaten food		○	○	○	○	○	○	○
Visually inspect.		○	○	○	○	○	○	○
Use calcium supplements 1 x / 2-3 day		○	○	○	○	○	○	○

NOTES:

WEEKLY CHECKLIST

WEEK OF

WEEKLY ACTIVITY

○ Clean glass

○ Top up substrate

○ Clean any decorative rocks, plants etc

○ Physically inspect

○ Weigh & record data

MONTHLY ACTIVITY

○ Remove & replace all substrate

HEALTH CHECKLIST

○ Active and alert

○ Eats regularly

○ Clear, bright eyes

○ Healthy skin

○ Clear nose and vent

NOTES:

HIGHLIGHT OF THE WEEK:

DAILY CHECKLIST

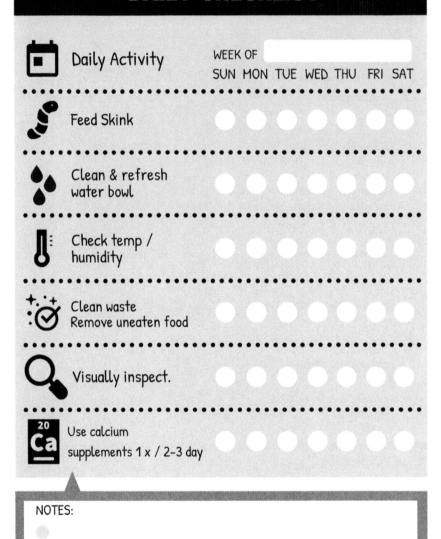

📅 Daily Activity

WEEK OF _____

SUN MON TUE WED THU FRI SAT

Feed Skink ○ ○ ○ ○ ○ ○ ○

Clean & refresh water bowl ○ ○ ○ ○ ○ ○ ○

Check temp / humidity ○ ○ ○ ○ ○ ○ ○

Clean waste Remove uneaten food ○ ○ ○ ○ ○ ○ ○

Visually inspect. ○ ○ ○ ○ ○ ○ ○

20 Ca Use calcium supplements 1 x / 2–3 day ○ ○ ○ ○ ○ ○ ○

NOTES:

WEEKLY CHECKLIST

WEEK OF

WEEKLY ACTIVITY

- ○ Clean glass
- ○ Top up substrate
- ○ Clean any decorative rocks, plants etc
- ○ Physically inspect
- ○ Weigh & record data

MONTHLY ACTIVITY

- ○ Remove & replace all substrate

HEALTH CHECKLIST

- ○ Active and alert
- ○ Eats regularly
- ○ Clear, bright eyes
- ○ Healthy skin
- ○ Clear nose and vent

NOTES:

HIGHLIGHT OF THE WEEK:

DAILY CHECKLIST

Daily Activity	WEEK OF						
	SUN	MON	TUE	WED	THU	FRI	SAT
Feed Skink	○	○	○	○	○	○	○
Clean & refresh water bowl	○	○	○	○	○	○	○
Check temp / humidity	○	○	○	○	○	○	○
Clean waste Remove uneaten food	○	○	○	○	○	○	○
Visually inspect.	○	○	○	○	○	○	○
Use calcium supplements 1 x / 2-3 day	○	○	○	○	○	○	○

NOTES:

WEEKLY CHECKLIST

WEEK OF

WEEKLY ACTIVITY

- Clean glass
- Top up substrate
- Clean any decorative rocks, plants etc
- Physically inspect
- Weigh & record data

MONTHLY ACTIVITY

- Remove & replace all substrate

HEALTH CHECKLIST

- Active and alert
- Eats regularly
- Clear, bright eyes
- Healthy skin
- Clear nose and vent

NOTES:

HIGHLIGHT OF THE WEEK:

DAILY CHECKLIST

Daily Activity	WEEK OF	SUN	MON	TUE	WED	THU	FRI	SAT
Feed Skink		○	○	○	○	○	○	○
Clean & refresh water bowl		○	○	○	○	○	○	○
Check temp / humidity		○	○	○	○	○	○	○
Clean waste Remove uneaten food		○	○	○	○	○	○	○
Visually inspect.		○	○	○	○	○	○	○
Use calcium supplements 1 x / 2-3 day		○	○	○	○	○	○	○

NOTES:

WEEKLY CHECKLIST

WEEK OF [   ]

WEEKLY ACTIVITY

○ Clean glass

○ Top up substrate

○ Clean any decorative rocks, plants etc

○ Physically inspect

○ Weigh & record data
[   ]

MONTHLY ACTIVITY

○ Remove & replace all substrate

HEALTH CHECKLIST

○ Active and alert

○ Eats regularly

○ Clear, bright eyes

○ Healthy skin

○ Clear nose and vent

NOTES:

HIGHLIGHT OF THE WEEK:

DAILY CHECKLIST

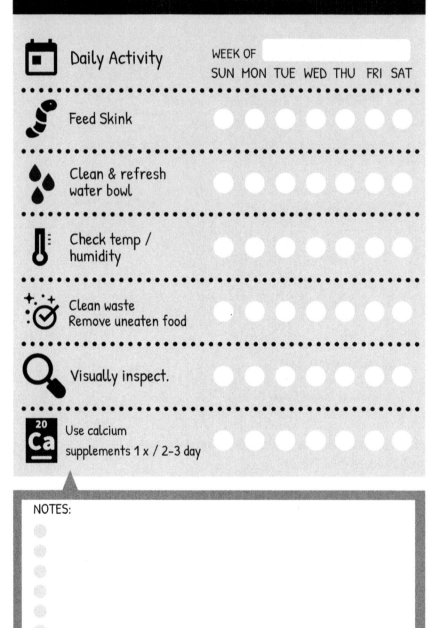

Daily Activity	WEEK OF						
	SUN	MON	TUE	WED	THU	FRI	SAT
Feed Skink	○	○	○	○	○	○	○
Clean & refresh water bowl	○	○	○	○	○	○	○
Check temp / humidity	○	○	○	○	○	○	○
Clean waste Remove uneaten food	○	○	○	○	○	○	○
Visually inspect.	○	○	○	○	○	○	○
Use calcium supplements 1 x / 2-3 day	○	○	○	○	○	○	○

NOTES:

WEEKLY CHECKLIST

WEEK OF

WEEKLY ACTIVITY

○ Clean glass

○ Top up substrate

○ Clean any decorative rocks, plants etc

○ Physically inspect

○ Weigh & record data

MONTHLY ACTIVITY

○ Remove & replace all substrate

HEALTH CHECKLIST

○ Active and alert

○ Eats regularly

○ Clear, bright eyes

○ Healthy skin

○ Clear nose and vent

NOTES:

HIGHLIGHT OF THE WEEK:

DAILY CHECKLIST

Daily Activity	WEEK OF						
	SUN	MON	TUE	WED	THU	FRI	SAT
Feed Skink	○	○	○	○	○	○	○
Clean & refresh water bowl	○	○	○	○	○	○	○
Check temp / humidity	○	○	○	○	○	○	○
Clean waste Remove uneaten food	○	○	○	○	○	○	○
Visually inspect.	○	○	○	○	○	○	○
Use calcium supplements 1 x / 2-3 day	○	○	○	○	○	○	○

NOTES:

WEEKLY CHECKLIST

WEEK OF [ ]

WEEKLY ACTIVITY

○ Clean glass

○ Top up substrate

○ Clean any decorative rocks, plants etc

○ Physically inspect

○ Weigh & record data
[ ]

MONTHLY ACTIVITY

○ Remove & replace all substrate

HEALTH CHECKLIST

○ Active and alert

○ Eats regularly

○ Clear, bright eyes

○ Healthy skin

○ Clear nose and vent

NOTES:

HIGHLIGHT OF THE WEEK:

DAILY CHECKLIST

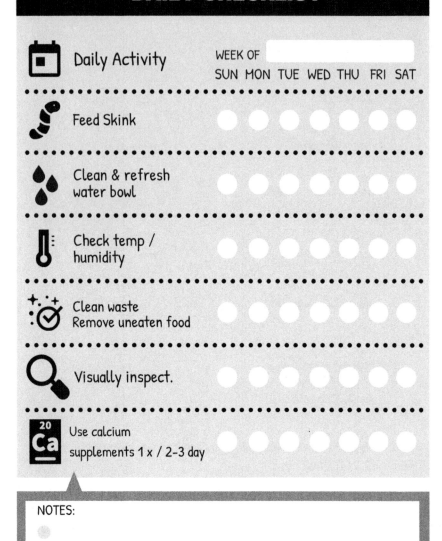

Daily Activity	WEEK OF						
	SUN	MON	TUE	WED	THU	FRI	SAT
Feed Skink	○	○	○	○	○	○	○
Clean & refresh water bowl	○	○	○	○	○	○	○
Check temp / humidity	○	○	○	○	○	○	○
Clean waste Remove uneaten food	○	○	○	○	○	○	○
Visually inspect.	○	○	○	○	○	○	○
Use calcium supplements 1 x / 2-3 day	○	○	○	○	○	○	○

NOTES:

WEEKLY CHECKLIST

WEEK OF _____

WEEKLY ACTIVITY

- ○ Clean glass
- ○ Top up substrate
- ○ Clean any decorative rocks, plants etc
- ○ Physically inspect
- ○ Weigh & record data
  _____

MONTHLY ACTIVITY

- ○ Remove & replace all substrate

HEALTH CHECKLIST

- ○ Active and alert
- ○ Eats regularly
- ○ Clear, bright eyes
- ○ Healthy skin
- ○ Clear nose and vent

NOTES:

HIGHLIGHT OF THE WEEK:

DAILY CHECKLIST

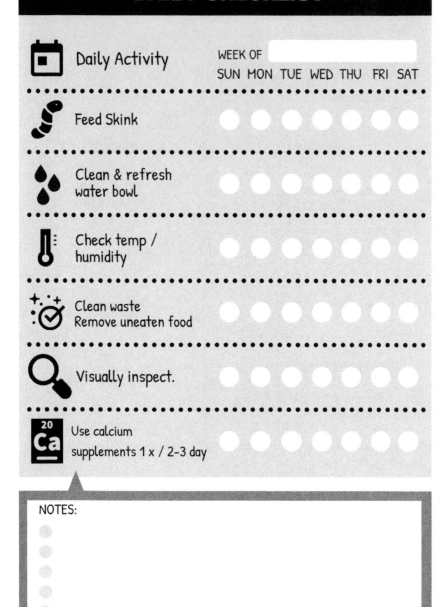

Daily Activity	WEEK OF	SUN	MON	TUE	WED	THU	FRI	SAT
Feed Skink		○	○	○	○	○	○	○
Clean & refresh water bowl		○	○	○	○	○	○	○
Check temp / humidity		○	○	○	○	○	○	○
Clean waste Remove uneaten food		○	○	○	○	○	○	○
Visually inspect.		○	○	○	○	○	○	○
Use calcium supplements 1 x / 2-3 day		○	○	○	○	○	○	○

NOTES:

WEEKLY CHECKLIST

WEEK OF _____

WEEKLY ACTIVITY

- ○ Clean glass
- ○ Top up substrate
- ○ Clean any decorative rocks, plants etc
- ○ Physically inspect
- ○ Weigh & record data
- ○ _____

MONTHLY ACTIVITY

- ○ Remove & replace all substrate

HEALTH CHECKLIST

- ○ Active and alert
- ○ Eats regularly
- ○ Clear, bright eyes
- ○ Healthy skin
- ○ Clear nose and vent

NOTES:

HIGHLIGHT OF THE WEEK:

DAILY CHECKLIST

Daily Activity	WEEK OF						
	SUN	MON	TUE	WED	THU	FRI	SAT
Feed Skink	○	○	○	○	○	○	○
Clean & refresh water bowl	○	○	○	○	○	○	○
Check temp / humidity	○	○	○	○	○	○	○
Clean waste Remove uneaten food	○	○	○	○	○	○	○
Visually inspect.	○	○	○	○	○	○	○
Use calcium supplements 1 x / 2-3 day	○	○	○	○	○	○	○

NOTES:

WEEKLY CHECKLIST

WEEK OF

WEEKLY ACTIVITY

- Clean glass
- Top up substrate
- Clean any decorative rocks, plants etc
- Physically inspect
- Weigh & record data

MONTHLY ACTIVITY

- Remove & replace all substrate

HEALTH CHECKLIST

- Active and alert
- Eats regularly
- Clear, bright eyes
- Healthy skin
- Clear nose and vent

NOTES:

HIGHLIGHT OF THE WEEK:

DAILY CHECKLIST

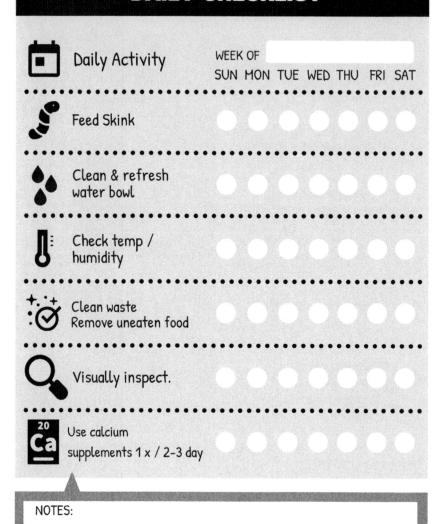

Daily Activity	WEEK OF	SUN	MON	TUE	WED	THU	FRI	SAT
Feed Skink		○	○	○	○	○	○	○
Clean & refresh water bowl		○	○	○	○	○	○	○
Check temp / humidity		○	○	○	○	○	○	○
Clean waste Remove uneaten food		○	○	○	○	○	○	○
Visually inspect.		○	○	○	○	○	○	○
Use calcium supplements 1 x / 2-3 day		○	○	○	○	○	○	○

NOTES:

WEEKLY CHECKLIST

WEEK OF [   ]

WEEKLY ACTIVITY

- Clean glass
- Top up substrate
- Clean any decorative rocks, plants etc
- Physically inspect
- Weigh & record data

[   ]

MONTHLY ACTIVITY

- Remove & replace all substrate

HEALTH CHECKLIST

- Active and alert
- Eats regularly
- Clear, bright eyes
- Healthy skin
- Clear nose and vent

NOTES:

HIGHLIGHT OF THE WEEK:

DAILY CHECKLIST

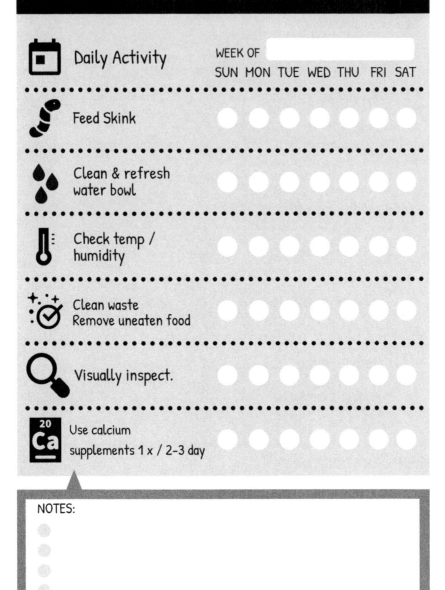

Daily Activity	WEEK OF	SUN	MON	TUE	WED	THU	FRI	SAT
Feed Skink		○	○	○	○	○	○	○
Clean & refresh water bowl		○	○	○	○	○	○	○
Check temp / humidity		○	○	○	○	○	○	○
Clean waste Remove uneaten food		○	○	○	○	○	○	○
Visually inspect.		○	○	○	○	○	○	○
Use calcium supplements 1 x / 2-3 day		○	○	○	○	○	○	○

NOTES:

WEEKLY CHECKLIST

WEEK OF [_____]

WEEKLY ACTIVITY

- ○ Clean glass
- ○ Top up substrate
- ○ Clean any decorative rocks, plants etc
- ○ Physically inspect
- ○ Weigh & record data [_____]

MONTHLY ACTIVITY

- ○ Remove & replace all substrate

HEALTH CHECKLIST

- ○ Active and alert
- ○ Eats regularly
- ○ Clear, bright eyes
- ○ Healthy skin
- ○ Clear nose and vent

NOTES:

HIGHLIGHT OF THE WEEK:

DAILY CHECKLIST

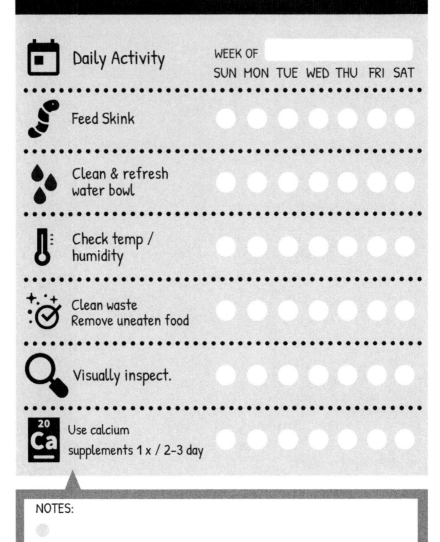

Daily Activity	SUN	MON	TUE	WED	THU	FRI	SAT
Feed Skink	○	○	○	○	○	○	○
Clean & refresh water bowl	○	○	○	○	○	○	○
Check temp / humidity	○	○	○	○	○	○	○
Clean waste Remove uneaten food	○	○	○	○	○	○	○
Visually inspect.	○	○	○	○	○	○	○
Use calcium supplements 1 x / 2-3 day	○	○	○	○	○	○	○

WEEK OF

NOTES:

WEEKLY CHECKLIST

WEEK OF

WEEKLY ACTIVITY

- Clean glass
- Top up substrate
- Clean any decorative rocks, plants etc
- Physically inspect
- Weigh & record data

MONTHLY ACTIVITY

- Remove & replace all substrate

HEALTH CHECKLIST

- Active and alert
- Eats regularly
- Clear, bright eyes
- Healthy skin
- Clear nose and vent

NOTES:

HIGHLIGHT OF THE WEEK:

DAILY CHECKLIST

Daily Activity	WEEK OF	SUN	MON	TUE	WED	THU	FRI	SAT
Feed Skink		○	○	○	○	○	○	○
Clean & refresh water bowl		○	○	○	○	○	○	○
Check temp / humidity		○	○	○	○	○	○	○
Clean waste Remove uneaten food		○	○	○	○	○	○	○
Visually inspect.		○	○	○	○	○	○	○
Use calcium supplements 1 x / 2-3 day		○	○	○	○	○	○	○

NOTES:

WEEKLY CHECKLIST

WEEK OF [_____]

WEEKLY ACTIVITY

- ○ Clean glass
- ○ Top up substrate
- ○ Clean any decorative rocks, plants etc
- ○ Physically inspect
- ○ Weigh & record data
  [_____]

MONTHLY ACTIVITY

- ○ Remove & replace all substrate

HEALTH CHECKLIST

- ○ Active and alert
- ○ Eats regularly
- ○ Clear, bright eyes
- ○ Healthy skin
- ○ Clear nose and vent

NOTES:

HIGHLIGHT OF THE WEEK:

DAILY CHECKLIST

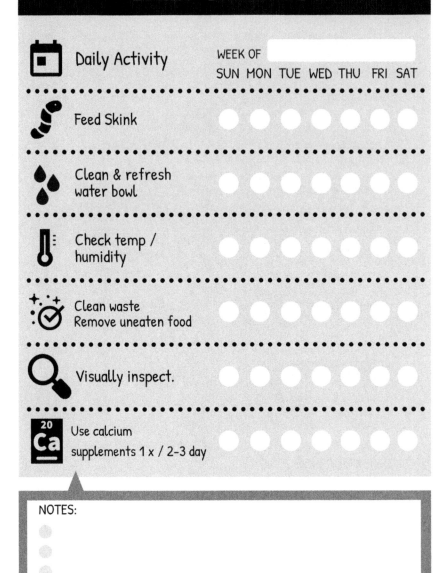

Daily Activity	WEEK OF						
	SUN	MON	TUE	WED	THU	FRI	SAT
Feed Skink	○	○	○	○	○	○	○
Clean & refresh water bowl	○	○	○	○	○	○	○
Check temp / humidity	○	○	○	○	○	○	○
Clean waste Remove uneaten food	○	○	○	○	○	○	○
Visually inspect.	○	○	○	○	○	○	○
Use calcium supplements 1 x / 2-3 day	○	○	○	○	○	○	○

NOTES:

WEEKLY CHECKLIST

WEEK OF _____

WEEKLY ACTIVITY

- ○ Clean glass
- ○ Top up substrate
- ○ Clean any decorative rocks, plants etc
- ○ Physically inspect
- ○ Weigh & record data
  _____

MONTHLY ACTIVITY

- ○ Remove & replace all substrate

HEALTH CHECKLIST

- ○ Active and alert
- ○ Eats regularly
- ○ Clear, bright eyes
- ○ Healthy skin
- ○ Clear nose and vent

NOTES:

HIGHLIGHT OF THE WEEK:

DAILY CHECKLIST

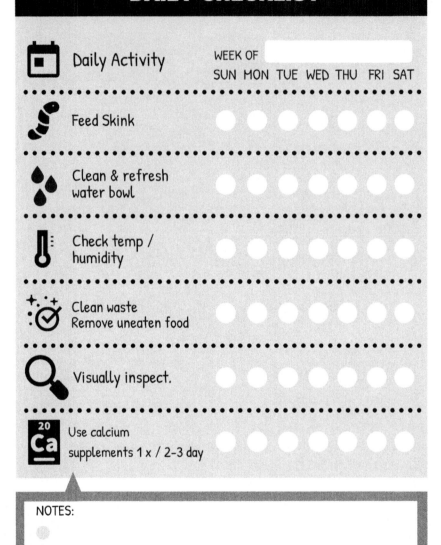

Daily Activity	WEEK OF	SUN	MON	TUE	WED	THU	FRI	SAT
Feed Skink		○	○	○	○	○	○	○
Clean & refresh water bowl		○	○	○	○	○	○	○
Check temp / humidity		○	○	○	○	○	○	○
Clean waste Remove uneaten food		○	○	○	○	○	○	○
Visually inspect.		○	○	○	○	○	○	○
Use calcium supplements 1 x / 2-3 day		○	○	○	○	○	○	○

NOTES:

WEEKLY CHECKLIST

WEEK OF

WEEKLY ACTIVITY

- Clean glass
- Top up substrate
- Clean any decorative rocks, plants etc
- Physically inspect
- Weigh & record data

MONTHLY ACTIVITY

- Remove & replace all substrate

HEALTH CHECKLIST

- Active and alert
- Eats regularly
- Clear, bright eyes
- Healthy skin
- Clear nose and vent

NOTES:

HIGHLIGHT OF THE WEEK:

DAILY CHECKLIST

Daily Activity	WEEK OF	SUN	MON	TUE	WED	THU	FRI	SAT
Feed Skink		○	○	○	○	○	○	○
Clean & refresh water bowl		○	○	○	○	○	○	○
Check temp / humidity		○	○	○	○	○	○	○
Clean waste Remove uneaten food		○	○	○	○	○	○	○
Visually inspect.		○	○	○	○	○	○	○
Use calcium supplements 1 x / 2-3 day		○	○	○	○	○	○	○

NOTES:

WEEKLY CHECKLIST

WEEK OF

WEEKLY ACTIVITY

○ Clean glass

○ Top up substrate

○ Clean any decorative rocks, plants etc

○ Physically inspect

○ Weigh & record data

MONTHLY ACTIVITY

○ Remove & replace all substrate

HEALTH CHECKLIST

○ Active and alert

○ Eats regularly

○ Clear, bright eyes

○ Healthy skin

○ Clear nose and vent

NOTES:

HIGHLIGHT OF THE WEEK:

DAILY CHECKLIST

Daily Activity	WEEK OF						
	SUN	MON	TUE	WED	THU	FRI	SAT
Feed Skink	○	○	○	○	○	○	○
Clean & refresh water bowl	○	○	○	○	○	○	○
Check temp / humidity	○	○	○	○	○	○	○
Clean waste Remove uneaten food	○	○	○	○	○	○	○
Visually inspect.	○	○	○	○	○	○	○
Use calcium supplements 1 x / 2-3 day	○	○	○	○	○	○	○

NOTES:

WEEKLY CHECKLIST

WEEK OF _____

WEEKLY ACTIVITY

○ Clean glass

○ Top up substrate

○ Clean any decorative rocks, plants etc

○ Physically inspect

○ Weigh & record data

_____

MONTHLY ACTIVITY

○ Remove & replace all substrate

HEALTH CHECKLIST

○ Active and alert

○ Eats regularly

○ Clear, bright eyes

○ Healthy skin

○ Clear nose and vent

NOTES:

HIGHLIGHT OF THE WEEK:

DAILY CHECKLIST

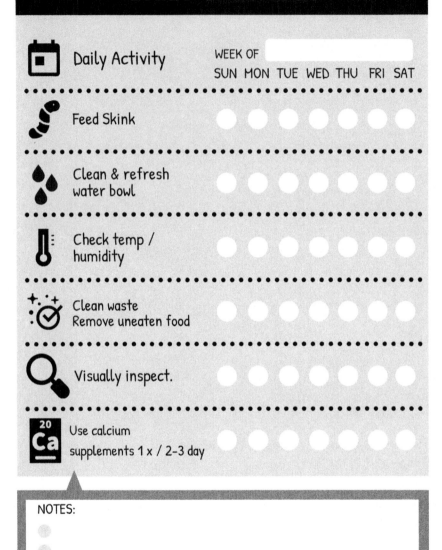

Daily Activity	WEEK OF	SUN	MON	TUE	WED	THU	FRI	SAT
Feed Skink		○	○	○	○	○	○	○
Clean & refresh water bowl		○	○	○	○	○	○	○
Check temp / humidity		○	○	○	○	○	○	○
Clean waste Remove uneaten food		○	○	○	○	○	○	○
Visually inspect.		○	○	○	○	○	○	○
Use calcium supplements 1 x / 2-3 day		○	○	○	○	○	○	○

NOTES:

WEEKLY CHECKLIST

WEEK OF [   ]

WEEKLY ACTIVITY

- ○ Clean glass
- ○ Top up substrate
- ○ Clean any decorative rocks, plants etc
- ○ Physically inspect
- ○ Weigh & record data
- [   ]

MONTHLY ACTIVITY

- ○ Remove & replace all substrate

HEALTH CHECKLIST

- ○ Active and alert
- ○ Eats regularly
- ○ Clear, bright eyes
- ○ Healthy skin
- ○ Clear nose and vent

NOTES:

HIGHLIGHT OF THE WEEK:

DAILY CHECKLIST

Daily Activity	WEEK OF	SUN	MON	TUE	WED	THU	FRI	SAT
Feed Skink		○	○	○	○	○	○	○
Clean & refresh water bowl		○	○	○	○	○	○	○
Check temp / humidity		○	○	○	○	○	○	○
Clean waste Remove uneaten food		○	○	○	○	○	○	○
Visually inspect.		○	○	○	○	○	○	○
Use calcium supplements 1 x / 2-3 day		○	○	○	○	○	○	○

NOTES:

WEEKLY CHECKLIST

WEEK OF

WEEKLY ACTIVITY

○ Clean glass

○ Top up substrate

○ Clean any decorative rocks, plants etc

○ Physically inspect

○ Weigh & record data

MONTHLY ACTIVITY

○ Remove & replace all substrate

HEALTH CHECKLIST

○ Active and alert

○ Eats regularly

○ Clear, bright eyes

○ Healthy skin

○ Clear nose and vent

NOTES:

HIGHLIGHT OF THE WEEK:

DAILY CHECKLIST

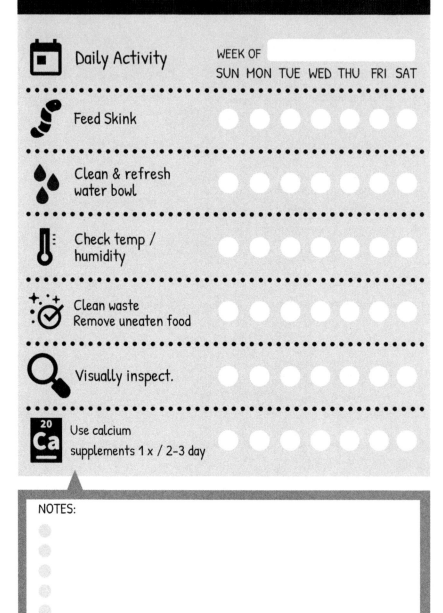

Daily Activity	WEEK OF						
	SUN	MON	TUE	WED	THU	FRI	SAT
Feed Skink	○	○	○	○	○	○	○
Clean & refresh water bowl	○	○	○	○	○	○	○
Check temp / humidity	○	○	○	○	○	○	○
Clean waste Remove uneaten food	○	○	○	○	○	○	○
Visually inspect.	○	○	○	○	○	○	○
Use calcium supplements 1 x / 2-3 day	○	○	○	○	○	○	○

NOTES:

WEEKLY CHECKLIST

WEEK OF

WEEKLY ACTIVITY

- ○ Clean glass
- ○ Top up substrate
- ○ Clean any decorative rocks, plants etc
- ○ Physically inspect
- ○ Weigh & record data

MONTHLY ACTIVITY

- ○ Remove & replace all substrate

HEALTH CHECKLIST

- ○ Active and alert
- ○ Eats regularly
- ○ Clear, bright eyes
- ○ Healthy skin
- ○ Clear nose and vent

NOTES:

HIGHLIGHT OF THE WEEK:

DAILY CHECKLIST

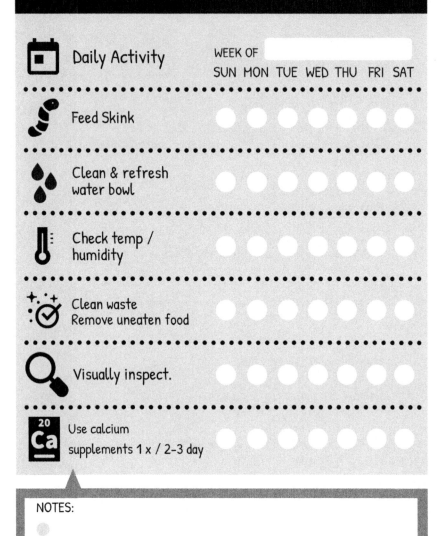

Daily Activity	WEEK OF	SUN	MON	TUE	WED	THU	FRI	SAT
Feed Skink		○	○	○	○	○	○	○
Clean & refresh water bowl		○	○	○	○	○	○	○
Check temp / humidity		○	○	○	○	○	○	○
Clean waste Remove uneaten food		○	○	○	○	○	○	○
Visually inspect.		○	○	○	○	○	○	○
Use calcium supplements 1 x / 2-3 day		○	○	○	○	○	○	○

NOTES:

WEEKLY CHECKLIST

WEEK OF

WEEKLY ACTIVITY

- Clean glass
- Top up substrate
- Clean any decorative rocks, plants etc
- Physically inspect
- Weigh & record data

MONTHLY ACTIVITY

- Remove & replace all substrate

HEALTH CHECKLIST

- Active and alert
- Eats regularly
- Clear, bright eyes
- Healthy skin
- Clear nose and vent

NOTES:

HIGHLIGHT OF THE WEEK:

DAILY CHECKLIST

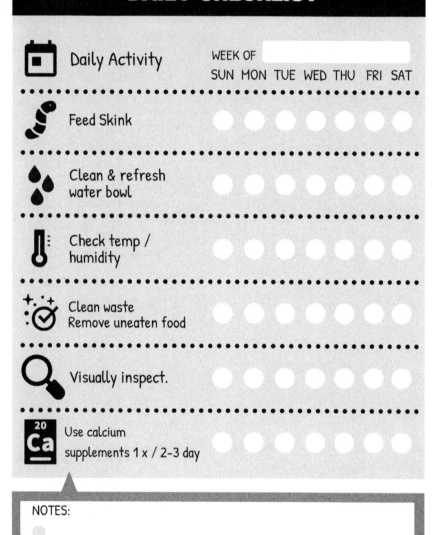

Daily Activity	WEEK OF						
	SUN	MON	TUE	WED	THU	FRI	SAT
Feed Skink	○	○	○	○	○	○	○
Clean & refresh water bowl	○	○	○	○	○	○	○
Check temp / humidity	○	○	○	○	○	○	○
Clean waste Remove uneaten food	○	○	○	○	○	○	○
Visually inspect.	○	○	○	○	○	○	○
Use calcium supplements 1 x / 2-3 day	○	○	○	○	○	○	○

NOTES:

WEEKLY CHECKLIST

WEEK OF

WEEKLY ACTIVITY

- ○ Clean glass
- ○ Top up substrate
- ○ Clean any decorative rocks, plants etc
- ○ Physically inspect
- ○ Weigh & record data

MONTHLY ACTIVITY

- ○ Remove & replace all substrate

HEALTH CHECKLIST

- ○ Active and alert
- ○ Eats regularly
- ○ Clear, bright eyes
- ○ Healthy skin
- ○ Clear nose and vent

NOTES:

HIGHLIGHT OF THE WEEK:

DAILY CHECKLIST

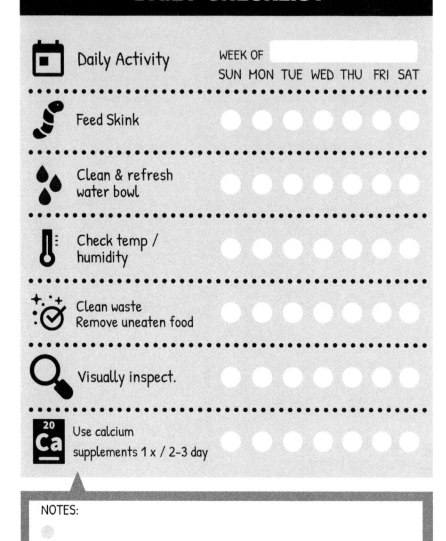

Daily Activity	WEEK OF	SUN	MON	TUE	WED	THU	FRI	SAT
Feed Skink		○	○	○	○	○	○	○
Clean & refresh water bowl		○	○	○	○	○	○	○
Check temp / humidity		○	○	○	○	○	○	○
Clean waste Remove uneaten food		○	○	○	○	○	○	○
Visually inspect.		○	○	○	○	○	○	○
Use calcium supplements 1 x / 2-3 day		○	○	○	○	○	○	○

NOTES:

WEEKLY CHECKLIST

WEEK OF _____

WEEKLY ACTIVITY

○ Clean glass

○ Top up substrate

○ Clean any decorative rocks, plants etc

○ Physically inspect

○ Weigh & record data

_____

MONTHLY ACTIVITY

○ Remove & replace all substrate

HEALTH CHECKLIST

○ Active and alert

○ Eats regularly

○ Clear, bright eyes

○ Healthy skin

○ Clear nose and vent

NOTES:

HIGHLIGHT OF THE WEEK:

DAILY CHECKLIST

Daily Activity	WEEK OF	SUN	MON	TUE	WED	THU	FRI	SAT
Feed Skink		○	○	○	○	○	○	○
Clean & refresh water bowl		○	○	○	○	○	○	○
Check temp / humidity		○	○	○	○	○	○	○
Clean waste Remove uneaten food		○	○	○	○	○	○	○
Visually inspect.		○	○	○	○	○	○	○
Use calcium supplements 1 x / 2-3 day		○	○	○	○	○	○	○

NOTES:

WEEKLY CHECKLIST

WEEK OF

WEEKLY ACTIVITY

- Clean glass
- Top up substrate
- Clean any decorative rocks, plants etc
- Physically inspect
- Weigh & record data

MONTHLY ACTIVITY

- Remove & replace all substrate

HEALTH CHECKLIST

- Active and alert
- Eats regularly
- Clear, bright eyes
- Healthy skin
- Clear nose and vent

NOTES:

HIGHLIGHT OF THE WEEK:

DAILY CHECKLIST

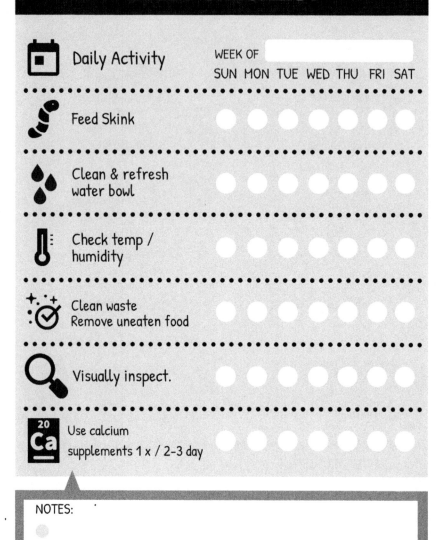

Daily Activity	WEEK OF
	SUN MON TUE WED THU FRI SAT
Feed Skink	○ ○ ○ ○ ○ ○
Clean & refresh water bowl	○ ○ ○ ○ ○ ○
Check temp / humidity	○ ○ ○ ○ ○ ○ ○
Clean waste Remove uneaten food	○ ○ ○ ○ ○ ○
Visually inspect.	○ ○ ○ ○ ○ ○
Use calcium supplements 1 x / 2-3 day	○ ○ ○ ○ ○ ○

NOTES:

WEEKLY CHECKLIST

WEEK OF _____

WEEKLY ACTIVITY

- ○ Clean glass
- ○ Top up substrate
- ○ Clean any decorative rocks, plants etc
- ○ Physically inspect
- ○ Weigh & record data
  _____

MONTHLY ACTIVITY

- ○ Remove & replace all substrate

HEALTH CHECKLIST

- ○ Active and alert
- ○ Eats regularly
- ○ Clear, bright eyes
- ○ Healthy skin
- ○ Clear nose and vent

NOTES:

HIGHLIGHT OF THE WEEK:

Printed in Great Britain
by Amazon